It Looks Like an Island…

Ralph Hawkins

It Looks Like an Island But Sails Away

Shearsman Books

First published in the United Kingdom in 2015 by
Shearsman Books
50 Westons Hill Drive
Emersons Green
BRISTOL
BS16 7DF

Shearsman Books Ltd Registered Office
30–31 St. James Place, Mangotsfield, Bristol BS16 9JB
(this address not for correspondence)

www.shearsman.com

ISBN 978-1-84861-420-8

ACKNOWLEDGEMENTS
My thanks go to those who have published some of these poems,
Tim Atkins, Anthony Barnett and Ian Brinton, Kelvin Corcoran,
Edmund Hardy, Peter Hughes, Peter Philpott.

CONTENTS

Gut

Down in the tubes like corridors of blood he lived. His name was Gut and his body had many rooms.

To the right was the Giant's room and his name was Git. Is Git a short giant? If Git and Gut have children it will be a miracle as they don't eat together. This would be the gustatorium. A windy palace of gables and false starts. Huge butterflies hung from Eve.

To the left, near St Pancras, Git swept the furniture room, which was bare and nearly naked of furniture, the odd fruit bowl which we now understand to be a type of quince. A few hung hams from the ceiling, a Bombay Bad Boy in the cupboard, a runaway from a poem which could be India by Slim Whitman.

When Gut moved he took his house with him. The underground and he were twins. This academics call travelling or motility. He followed the map of life for hours hoping to arrive. Plutarch arguing that some animals are more intelligent than others.

Space is a place in point. Maybe it's the extremes that keep us going. Git has copulated and seeded many times. Gut just keeps on growing. Marx tells us that Man has become denatured. My mind is nude on a carousel.

The mercredoir has sugarloaf walls and plasticine furniture, inflammable at high temperatures. Git almost always seeking the Comrade perfect.

Reg of Orleans

Jeanne was not a common termagant,
not a harlot, not a witch, not a blasphemer,
no more an idolater than the Pope himself

The vanished limbless
on vermicelli millet fields, splayed cysts,
cracked bone and tar-oil

golden wheatless

perhaps a copper-green in oil or the
mordant gold of a halo-lamp

there are forensic traces of red on purpled lips

perhaps a burning of books

Reg went to Rome maybe on the 12:18

got ill on Milanese salami and applied ointment
(healing balm oil)

wearing a rayed hello with a star

sustained on bread dipped in milk or wine

2.

The Snow White car backfires in revolvo
Spotty faced with a Glock 17
Stripped in the waste, near Barearsed
A golden winged Nike on his fleet feet

His victim's head laid halo upon his lap

Other views… gold trimmed with ermine in rings of flame

                    to the left
lemon trees
                    and to the right bright Orange

a bird with two coats
one male the other gives a spotted appearance

the tunic the hats the dress and
the blue of a river

the Volvo has a decorative trim
a horizontal of wheels and crescent moons (moans?)

apparently the trees refer to *m & f*

tattooed on a forearm

3.

Egg Foo Yung in Poplar
        the hills behind (calendar wall painting
                    month of April)
        are flooded (terraced)
with the light of an eastern dawn
the sky ultramarine (Genoa) – pupil of Pisano

Other meals:
Jeanne's bread dipped in wine with silent letters
Jimmy's stifado (Soho)
Jerome's habit, cape and ungilded halo
the leaves picked out in malachite and
tin lead yellow

there seems to be a pentimento in the oculus

hot green chillies
lemon grass

tiny fish hatched and swimming pool in the soup

stuffed

pimento and octopus

Ray's light from March
with intermittent roundels of
blue with white palm

4.

head of haired beardless man

head of a haired bearded man

much of what I thought

first one fin and then another
he counts up his 'sins' on mini hands

a dish of dauphinoise

blue belted above the waist
birds with tiny wings (robins with scraves!)
flock in a field of carnations (dianthus)

his hair cute parted

MOST WANTED MAN

or Jeanne 1431

rays gilded with blue spots in hot water tub

a star on her shoulder
and the rings on her finger
in what appears to be a red lake

raindrop sprays appear – transparent

am I too

in green underpants

showing the Man of (constant) Sorrow

5.

This time mussing / musing about hair

sit and do nothing
gaze into silence

she wears a black shirt
          over a robin redbreast vest
                    which is buttoned at the neck

the weather too is fair
          to golden-chest-nut brown
                    with many knots and floors
                              in her face

Line one: your earlobes and wen

a baby's skin
a fine waist

to be continued

fitter, trimmer, flatter

the bird

flies

out of her mouth

flames

6.

Jeanne hangs her vest to dry
1430
near the end now

egg on wood – snow on bare trees

the bed head and the bed end (the good beginning)
are decorated with music makers (angels)
under an arcade of possible ways to live – given the circumstances

there is scattered flake loss in the fire place

aesthetes moving from the city and going into the desert

from above we cross patchwork fields
tiny florists (birthdays, weddings and funerals)
and small castellated towns

the mountains are peeped snow-capped
Snow White and ethereal on the horizon

roses grow from bud to flower fairly light (fairy alights?)
on the tree

a dove coming out of Ray's
Salmon dancing weaving (rays don't dance)
pink on top of the cake platter

blood red icing sugar------------------one method of writing here
is to re-use composition(s) and motifs
for example the bed
its removal is usually of great significance to torture
(Hunger, L'instinct de mort, Jeanne la Pucelle etc)

lettieri (night beds) and *lettuci* (day beds)
are decorated with intarsia

Anne's bed has a blue canopy with golden stars

hers is the birth of a boy
the window open onto a fenced garden

flames lick from the sun

Ray's face alight

while another enters with a
terracotta potty on her head

7.

His workshop was in Piazza Santo Stefano
near the Ponte Vecchio

a formulaic and derivative artist

but he invented boil in the bag and French sticks to
sustain him – a margarita sky from Mexico (?)

there was a mystic marriage at hand (O
happy days in World's End)

and there are 3 golden balls

where he broke his rod (orb?)
wearing blue with gold stars and pink ribs

Apollonia lost her teeth before she was burned

lived with snakes and small devils

a chicken wing visible below a cloud

a kicking *c* from a poem by Joe Ceravalo
from which I now float like a white bear

The History of Inventions

Twin Bedouins star fixation from an old photo
with a green lacquer over the sky's rim
the height of Nile water
also sparkles
she wears rhinestones from a necklace like a cowboy
behind a pale blue film or veil

a hundred pieces of string
(to tie up the Vest)
dripped in yellow sunshine form clusters of nut gold

women in the West? God, Saloon and the Brothel

a choker and a dress with cheese puff sleeves

she was an aristocrat by birth and a ballerina by profession

Leopold II
the aging bon-vivant of Belgium
always tinkering worked hard at first on the
Light Bulb
and then the
Fuse Box

which like sleep and thought make the night disappear

Other Inventions

a wren's nest a ball
termite concrete (Mali)
mole hill spittoons (line 10)
match stick beaver (!)
spider gusset webbing
the honey of a bee
we take our caves with us when we go (tortoise quote)

Jesus Gong

In the midst of my egg (Cone-Head the barber) is a gong
And in my gong my ma, mon père et mes enfants
They are scrambled together with love and bacon
Overt time has fattened me (egg-bound)
The sun has bronzed me off
There are pigmy doors within my ancient crimes
And as for world accord I continue to stream
Alas I have grown layer on layer of thick shell-rind
If anyone intimate knows me they will know I have marrow-fat knees
I am a gong and my ears are full of cotton-buds

The Poems of
Abakan Tatar

the light weaves water into ice from
the sea where 8 rivers run

a series of pontoons protons and plateaus

the Kalmucks neural firing
contains preservatives and invention (intervention?)
apricot hills, mountain peach, arboreal rice

here at Earth's top you can see
the glistening world – lights and traffic in endless chains
of rice bead grains

there the settled and unsettled live in a state of
many positions (positrons)

2.

Kultic poets drew on unusual landscapes
visited by early explorers travelling
the Travnik highway

the first through virgin snow in search of booty (beauty?)

tracked by wolves
they left litters of having been poop

their male-coats studded
their shields shining waxen with arctic ice

those believing in the house knew its walls would
crack on such foundations

3.

in another poem a cosmic
          Lenin's death is viewed as an event which
disturbs the course of nature

Joe Meek dictates! Telstar

he heard voices

every house bugged

Ulrike working for the Stasi?

where the Tsar of the Sea's home is only an *izba* or hut

William dictating to Dot on craggy hillsides

a kind of hovel unlike the houses of rakes
ceilings painted like the sky

the Kults have little experience
of this because they dwell in remote parts

their doors hangings of bear pelt

but 7 men could not open them
the bolts to their minds made of larch

Joe could read the future in *Kutune Shirka*

he lived over a handbag shop all his
life until he received supernatural promptings
to travel aboard

zigzagged as fence rain
and catch a golden otter

4.

put cream and sugar in it
        this is Kara-Kirghiz tea

Russian tea is different

Russian pots do it in the stockyard with a trowel

turning east to pray

Lenin began his day like any other *bogatyr* with tea
(not White Russian)

however Lenin did not say morning prayers

Dawn's roseate fingers before
him blood blistered

the Emperor is lying in honey-mead (sweet-tongued by Rosie Dawn)
and spiced pear fixed to the end of the moon (a moan?)

he's laced a pot with linen (?) seed

her breath the evening's fragrance sends
scent to heaven there

Happy Whale Fat Smile

I want to laugh
but my ribs have cracked
Now how shall I travel

I struck ice
I laugh because they say it is melting
but it hurts

It rose up and struck me

Now I am covered by snow cloud
I touch my whale charm
Will I be able to fly like plovers

2.

I know what I want to write
But the words are on folded paper like a butterfly
It is so often difficult

You are a fish I can feel on the line through an ice hole

I laugh because they say the ice is melting

Why is it so difficult to write when the butterfly is made of snow

Your ears will burn and
Your heart will melt
Your lips a balm of warmth

When summer comes the snow butterfly will slip past me
like melting ice

3.

There will always be great men
Keng is one of them from the land of Telknam
There are strange tribes there
driving trucks of guano to foreign depots

flying foxes in the trees

there are men with fish heads
and more with big bows
in the anteroom they write Keng's name in history

the poor wait at the river bank
stars shimmering watering the skies with fireflies

Herds of auroch and deer are mountains of meat walking
moving from Africa to France through Spain
all with Keng's name on them

4.

We paddle towards the splinters of white ice

our paddle makes a cautious sound

my eyes catch the discoidal inflorescence of a sunflower

We journey towards the centre of our being (survival) (on thin ice)

read paddle as reed

on thin ice one must endeavour to be an equal

I saw a caribou with a white bear

I saw a moon man with a cave girl

the furthest stars look down upon and melt your heart

5.

poems are made through a process of fragmentation
and integration, compound images (multifocal) are formed

a man with zigzag legs

the blend is at once geometric and iconic

here people (words) feel themselves turning into animals

the cave girl

what stage of consciousness is this

she has stars painted all over her face
'o heavens'

they dab stripes on her arms
they dab spots on her stripes

read Murdock's Ethnographic Atlas

6.

let me do nothing but dab the breeze on my face

I will fly away through the hole in the melting ice

you made me walk on land under the water

huge fish the colour of ptarmigan fly down there

7.

the discodial rays of the flowers turn in the wind

where do they point

the flowers seem to waver to and fro-ing in the dab of the breeze

what does the branch point to

that the fruit might be red and acid

their sprays blow in the wind almost sea foam hanging down

the blackwood blooms are falling they give off a sweet blossom

parrots have ripped them

the dabs of falling blossom one by one look like bees
in varying degrees of interdependence and coalescence

8.

In Eremotherium
the hills are ridged and channelled their
contours folded and sinuous
Beyond Copper Town the light stretches
Warping it towards the sea
Here you will find the little boat of my mind

Once in Rhinoceros broad gaps replaced
narrow cols, jutted crags
figured on the contour lines
the so-called crochet and anticrochet
of our very being

In Sinohippus erosion goes
no further than the summit of several cusps
to the south the clouds change into
the sea as they swell
the peaks are wrapped in magnolia
where twilight makes the lovers beautiful

9.

There are carp of a thousand colours
There are thousands of carp in the river
They hide in the waters in which you swim

The gaze of the deer hides in the peppermint
The gaze of the deer in the thousands of mottled light
You hide in the leaves in which you are surrounded

10.

Leif was a good man
a circus performer and a
part-time magician

his brother was a good hunter
he always came home with a beauty (?)
happy whale fat smile and joy on his face

sometimes they had to hide(!) as sheep
or goats in the land of the enemy -
hills and valleys full of the first
wet moist snow

once they had to eat
the dog of the circus

11.

in a dream a dolphin
came out of the open sea
and walked upon the land

this means you will become a hunter
and buy *Harpoon Weekly*

maybe drive a grit-lorry in winter

or maybe the President
of a Democratic republic

you may redistribute wealth
(one of the old dolphin school)

and now the sky as lemon as a lozenge
with a strawberry-coloured sheik

12.

a mood has me count plums on a tree

but it's Wednesday and the sky
is a plum pudding made with
cloud covered whipped eggs

from another source I recall a white bear
by the edge of an ice-floe

I laugh when they say the ice is melting

the sky is full of rain-slush
and a purple fish the colour
of a plum-wound in the water

13.

of one of the enemy
they made a bag of leaves
and stewed him over a fire

when the minister speaks
from a tin of sweetmeats

he speaks with a barbecued tongue

he holds himself straight, repeatedly

he is not complicit with complicity

he knows nothing of sharp sticks
or poisoned arrows

yet his teeth shine like arrow heads
bleach-white in the sun

pliers, razor blades, electrodes

in his white shirt and garrotted tie
he must remain forever unchidden

14.

Leif has a great desire to use
his magic root, stick-stem, wizard rod

this is the road to Yakulta
Yeast writes poems there

pies rise in price*

with it he will catch a dog and skew it

or out on the firm ice he will wait for flat fish

if he has a surplus he can sell it and move west

*the fruit plump at the end of the spray
a spray of stars in the autumn sky

the plump bird at the end of the stars
the squirrel moving from having been to having been

15.

here is the honey-woman
climbing up a stick
to the neck

Pop gathers moss for wicks

a blow-pipe made of bamboo
green lizards on thorn trees

his poisoned arrow

Debbie the honey-woman bee
has long hands

Pop yearns for them

she swims past in the sea

cave-girl

full of purple stars

she has no children, only a poor dog
and nothing else

this is all Pop knows of the honey-woman

16.

a cold wind runs through the cane-grass
acacias bedecked with white flower-buds
he bends her back
her hair flows in the cold air
making a love-nest on the carpet
turning on the heater in the car-port

17.

The Human Cycle

A man runs and the animal eats him

A man flies and he crashes (early petroglyph)

A man swims and the shark eats him

_____

There are people with too much power

They get their power from their teeth

They set snares in their grins

_____

Soon young men will want wombs

And women cocks so they can piss at different angles

Pleasant things are always sensual

18.

white flowers grow in the melting snow-fields
the tree has been here for a long time
the Indians surround the hut in the clearing
my snow-hut is high in the alps
an old elephant could crush my hut
little birds live in the stringy-bark tree
the pygmies have little huts, of moss & fern,
they do not want silvery ghosts to wander through them
bats who will supper on their blood
when the moon shines on my snow-hut it
lances the mountains with silver ice beams
they say dead stars are the friends of ghosts
the tree falls into a river
it causes a great commotion – a rumbling in the clearing
like an echo in the mountains
all the branches are lost – dead, swept aside
and you lie there as if you are only sleeping
you have gone to white and bone
we all go to bone and bones go white

19.

when she left
she took my last jar of honey
(the first sound may well have been the smacking of honeyed lips)
and my digging stick

but she lies in the ground now
and will dig no more (see previous poem)

she won't lie by the fire
or gaze at the hearth our figures like trees
in our limb to limb

or comb out her honey-coloured hair

.

20.

what is it that blocks our way

at sea it is the whale

it looks like an island but it sails away

there is no land beyond this without roots which go back

it is always sailing away

was there dance before song

the smacking of lips

or image before spoken word

as we paddle we see it it is fading away

21.

to have love and plenty is a good thing

but I am not a good hunter or lover

seals toy with me, crabs pinch me and bears chase me away

dogs lead me nowhere over the ice

women lead me nowhere over the ice

they say that the world is ending

that my bed will be empty

and my table will be bare

22.

one final song

on the ice surface sitting over the fishing hole

I laugh because they say the world is melting

maybe we'll leave it as birds

it can't be repeated

snow falls like goose down from pillows

I usually make a hole in the wrong place in the ice

Fifteen Rode

Fifteen rode off
east over the river's custard moon

for clothes they had Ox
which the boy burned and scraped off

they looked after the meat
cut in slivers, sausaged and cured

what dwelt in their minds

there must have been one who
never spoke ill, never threatened
and had a wood(en) stove

2.

Bergitte and Ejnar had their flowers

like lit torches
riding a horse through starnight

they heard the water crash on the meadow way

the earth and sky revolving

the horses ran through a ring of fields

mountains lit up by a custard moon

he lay down in his duck

and if wise may choose never to come out of it

3.

Does a race have roots?

and his self doesn't exist without her

the two become one and the one become many

There was a man named after the son
of an old Bolshevik (now there is glacial shelf stacking in *Iceland*)

Bergitte opened a flower booth (*The Belt of Orion*)

a quick dictionary rampage brought in the cherry and the guava

trout from Denmark (close by)

some chick peas and braised lamb

the ice-slope, the angel-cake

some seed, some not

Bergitte removed the bracelet from her arm

to Ejnar it was worth 12 hundred ells (eels?) of
stripped homespun

4.

east across Helgeå

a soup made of pigs' balls

a town in snowflakes less than dust

one with his heart (hurt?) in his mouth

cherry lips behind the hills
cherry pips and thyme seeds on her leg(gins)

and tears from those clouds that hang
over us from time to time

when he is thinking of you

that time when this day is done

5.

[50% of psychopaths have lived in California at some point in their lives]

Knut (an early spelling)
shot him with a dicky bow (!)

50 welsh dressers live in California

Kol Egilsson had a go at Kellogs

a yello ola yoke setting (hardboiled)

Knut (Viggo Mortensen) removed them from
the land of the living (room)

see what Eric set off in Greenland

the history of violence

6.

the Thingmen went with him
(they were all in league with him
in limbo) in a fitted out ship

in life said Leif there is good
wind and bad

people go off of course

but the good ones got up some quails egg

make a farm like Ammonites with Anemones

blue in spring with showers of rain

Thingmen can change heads and eels in shops

they are among us now

they hack off rivers at the thigh

and stop the growth of grain for food

7.

Kolinka poked at Björn
"We'll go far east across the mountains to Thingamajig"

Kolinka packed a parcel down for a bed cramped like snowflakes
which fell like phosphorous in twists and twirls and spirals into
the water of the glacier by the farms of the Ammonite

for a moment everything was panphysical

puffin larders, buds diced in nut-oil

spears of land and shoulders of blunt rock

Kolinka said to Björn "It is time to rest your brain,

have stuffed hearts"

it was an all lava landscape

Kolinka lay an egg puffin under an overhang

and in the distance packed horses

looked both pretty and glum feeding on lyme-grass

they stayed three starfull nights by the belt of Orion

they travelled east to Helgeå

where they finally met with open heart surgery

whose chief surgeon had a very blonde wife

Mouth to Mouth

Make sick or sting Southern Fire Ant on a scale of pain

names of airplanes Yellowjacket, Bullet Ant, Mosquito! Drones

thoughts sparkle into voices on sting of instigation

hydrant, enkindler or inflamer

or out of itself like a honey bee

ringing in my ears

In Indonesia bee larvae are eaten as a companion to rice. It is mixed with coconut meat and steamed in banana leaves.

Palpable mysterium

the stars boiling clash

or separates itself in itself

a liquid body corpus glowing waxing

sinks, the chiefest of metals is a liquid star

there is a similitude, likeness

Illicium anisatum

swine flu bumps up the spice of life

Gulab Jal عرق گلاب *Rose Water is sprinkled an essence to welcome guests*

loco lobo loca

and it is the tincture which tinctures the body

which draws it to itself

proceeding from the mouth to the mouth (*boca a boca*)

the one is not the other but the two
(the two bee pendent) (the to be pendent) become one in

a strange fire and not so strange

a fire needs only itself

outgrowing, breathing

a sting to life

Decoction is a method of extraction, of boiling herbal or plant material, which may include stems, roots, bark and rhizomes.

there is no salvation in lust

or death or immobility!

changing tack: I never wanted a tambourine nor one who lay like a lute

a good man strikes his hidden instrument

it's as if one is surrounded by a thousand causeways

and I stand still with an upright, full and unfeigned desire

soon I will have a stronger body

with which to labor and if lucky

depart

being entertained nightly by angels (trumpets) and loving it

Brugmansia are large shrubs or small trees, reaching heights of 3–11 m, with tan, slightly rough bark. They are known as Angel's Trumpets. They are long-lived with pendulous, not erect, flowers that have no spines on their fruit.

dumb, senseless governments

virtue or efficacy?

the body politic lies

they wrestle and seethe

a gross stone in the head, seething

seizes on (like a bird) to shoot or to twig

all the money (the growth) in a bag or sack

Being, material and food all belong to nature

I still don't understand *Free Willy*

It is only the higher being – according to or after

On a furious wheel in a small pool head

Around and around the faithful question

to be led through a riddle unknowingly

"close your eyes...then you'll see it,
along with everything it contains"

it begets itself for us out of itself

and he set his desire upon anger (not Buddha then)

that was one thing and behind one thing was another

until it was all bagged up with a body

The path of the zipper may be J or D shaped

Blended

there are curdled texts in the air

or in wedlock blended "the clouds are numbered"

variously trumpeted nymphets

~~in quest of receiving what we are after~~

to make a living   of discovery

there are motifs running through her dress

the waters of turned into perfume   attar of

so that confections are made only in essence

You always carry a bag or sack with you –

it mirrors it

empty the contents of your mind and

it is called self wrestling

all governance is a lie

a green shoot carries with it a gallows

a dead fat corpus or two, a twig a bird, a branch of being

roots off into riot   the law stolid

a choice between virtue and efficacy

as slippery as wrestling with mercury

It was said that the cosmos was fashioned of three spiritual substances: the tria prima of mercury, sulfur, and salt.

light ether is said to bring virtues

or nausea — the give and take and yields

of the market, unseen vegetables still yet to be had,

profitability — they say now that camels'

milk will be good for me they say

you carry your likeness inside

if everything is the now and outside then we are in trouble

I will take off all my clothes and do the camel dance

a khaki colour

the text glances forth to a night of riot and separation

blue moons a kind of voice or harmony wrestling

with perceptual shape and reconfiguration

the essence of which is grounded in sensation

the anguished love of two Bees of one buzzing

one said it was a ship, one said nothing and the third

said it was a house with a missing chimney

but it was a moon like a blue cheese and his beard was peppered grey

if you change one letter it is a board floating on the sea

By Camel Thorn

see horses in words, the bees in combs and arches in

imagine a world without

a cold plum in space (two pimples, a gastric band, a shower curtain)

viaducts across a ruined cosmic empire

all these "things" we talk of and discuss heartfelt

everything we seemingly need (sweet peas and gnomes)

resistance and consent of ethical demands

_____

popped off a few names on my *hit list*
by the camel thorn and chinaberry and the fake alarm clock
I do keep taking the pills
one for a cuckoo twitch — a capsule — where once there was a life
of the mind (which one) with its built in self torture
woodworm, spigots, giant caterpillars

What is the goal of psychoanalysis? (quote)

There, up in the mountains, in the snow leading an authentic life
all of us in our place

drowsy on wormwood

one for asleep and one for a wake

and one for a shopping list

_____

Linne de Passe 2:30 of an afternoon count your blessings

I'm covered in Dove

ready to sink into my medication, a few chants and ring tones

as white as snow and as Fifi as clouds my memory is unsettled

was it you only a minute ago

whose sails are now on the decrease

dead calm, autochthonic, bill and cooing

ave maria with a little dribble

o madre o madre on a controlled diet

_____

tenderly with a kiss at the end (it's an x) of a letter (Mr to Mrs Adams?)

what we have here is an asymmetric cheese

an old (x) asteroid sucked in by gravity

bed linen on the line, you grow older by the split second

see the wind in the wind-sock, a pair of tights, a ladder, a goose fair

lots of loose-leaf fluttering of memoria, a blow of sorts,

a lot of waving before the compressional collapse

who fathered these goats who tethered their wills

off in the wind of design (no pun)

---

nothing there (ambiguous?), a diver in a lake, a dark angel

do you recall Burt Lancaster somewhere (Cleveland?)

neither do I

someone wrote misery all over our condition enhanced by protein
supplements

in the night sky, en el lago an embolism

a pharmacopeia of ideals would be enough to dispense with certain ideas

transcommunal knowledge of the enemy, a leviathan, mild hallucination,
mind cramps

but in the fields (so there is something?) butterwort and Daisy

I have taken them for 16 years, chronic skin troubles, as well as flatulence
and heart

burn

_____

la lluvia y los caminos

odd named trees in the garden
arbol del thule (the stoutest tree in the world)

silk worm sales, waves of indignation

how we love here in the northern hemisphere our short summer weather
bringing relief from the rain and snow of winter

a sprout of angels from a sea storm, the push of religion over blocked roads

arbol de la noche triste, gloomy night tree, bringing smallpox,

psychopaths given free reign (what we've got we've got by losing everything)

gentle traveller, spiritual pilgrim

on bobbin boats

pushy through the jungle his great buttocks heaved

"It is not known how long he was among them"

a policy of piss, slash and torture

———————————————————————

what use is grass? cows like it

I have a vision of one so young at the meat counter where there was much pressing of tongues

and one of straw

why do they garner fame and/or notoriety (cows?)

there's not a lot going on in his head that he doesn't know about

shaped like an egg on its way to the stars

in the book Bill was always in bed with a lemon

and his new fiscal policy was about to rob more people of what they
            didn't have

fat humpty dumpties writing poems they'd stolen from drains

a convenience store close by

dumpsites

depressives

_____

the earth's apple tinted dawn
ready to burst upon us once more or not
mujer ante el sol

and in the air wondering if the oxygen mask works

balloons for birthdays

cot toys

a huge icicle forms in Iceland

you've come with the tofu set wrapped in a bear skin
(an unhappy taxidermist)

blinis with caviar, Irish stew and the Queen of Puddings

it's gone down now

there are three starlets
and one cosmetic box

tinsel tinkle

apple turns to peach and they both laugh

Percy speaks a few words of Arabic
Mrs Zobel always keeps her eggs in the same basket and
Can now turn on her television remotely
Last winter her children moved to Florida
Why did her children move to Florida?

How often does Percy turn on the television?
Little did he realize what was in store for him when he entered the girls'
         room
Percy wasn't born yesterday?
I find it hard to believe that Percy really knows Arabic

Crossing the street against the light Percy was almost hit by a taxi
The moon came out from behind a cloud and he did not see it
Last Saturday was Percy's birthday
Olga and Melanie are quiet girls. What were they doing in their room?
Mr Crump, a neighbour has gone to Burma.
Mrs Zobel dropped an ostrich egg on the kitchen floor.
It made a big splash.
The girls said they felt rejected and disheartened.
It is difficult to believe Percy tried speaking Arabic to them.

Yesterday Percy left for Saigon
That month the war got serious
There once was a good bakery in Gia Long Street
Percy went into the street.
Miss Ba has bought a new blue dress
Lan's dress is leaf green. Such a dress is beautiful.
Miss Ba fried 3 chicken eggs.
It was Percy's birthday. He was happy.
He had a nut cluster, some oranges and a special boiled bird.
Lan had 6 shrimp.
Mr Ba is now in Gia Long Street looking for bread.
The white dress Mrs Zobel wore was her mother's
5 bamboo plants
Lan describes Mr Ba's fishing boat. It has gone for more shrimp.
Mr Ba thinks Gia Long Street is very messy and very smelly.
A goose flies.
A perfectly happy person has a vase full of their favourite flowers
Hoa's dress of perfect blue is in the closet
As now she has no reason to wear it.

Mrs Zobel almost always had an extra amount of eggs thanks to her
   chickens
A cluster of birds in the evening mock orange
The short lived life of a moth
Miss Hoa never eats eggs
Is Miss Lan Mrs Ba's daughter
Mrs Ba gave birth to Miss Lan in 1940
I can only dream of my previous wives
Why did I order such a large meal
There is plenty for everyone
The orchid on the table is a beautiful species of flower
Some people eat very quickly, some are desirous and some mean well
Mrs Ba gave Lan a bag for the leftovers
Intrigued the field leads to several buffalo
After we walk into the garden
One day passes into another
One lifetime
It's late now
Mr Ba stands besides his first wife's grave, one flower
And the Gods to protect us
The state to provide housing
There is gloom everywhere in this winter weather.

These flowers are for Parviz
Now his house has been destroyed
Sara is obliged to work,
                          she no longer has a home
The children are forced to work
It is necessary that the house be rebuilt
Sara will be forced to work

Parviz's house has been destroyed
The village has been destroyed

It is necessary that the children be looked after by their grandparents

Some children are orphans

Sara does not want the doctor to examine her
Parviz would have persuaded the doctor to examine Sara

Mary believed Bill to be at home
But Bill had gone off with Rose
John sat alone in his car, he shouldn't drink

The pair of them may be singing and dancing right now
There will be no complaints from Rose
John tends to lack insight, care and knowledge of the other
He is careless with money

He has to drive all the way to Stuggart for a biscuit conference
Rose is his ex, she still lives in Stuggart
He is thinking he is at the scene of the "crime" now

Mary's life is a mess

There is so little we know of what is in another's refrigerator

Hoping to be reliant, ethical, true, a good parent and in love

Fuck the conference

Mary told John they ought to wash themselves / each other
But John believes keeping his sex life under control is
necessary for promotional success

what about, Fuck the conference?
and fuck everybody in attendance

Don't fuck with Mary

Mary told John washing each other would be fun.
John washed, shaved and dressed himself
Fuck John thought Mary

John promised Fred he would shave for the conference.

Bizan knows he will read a book, many books
but which book will Bizan read.
Bizan drives through what was once his friend's village.
He could not recall if Parviz told him who he liked to kiss
Sara liked to kiss Parviz when they were alone and the children slept.
They slept huddled together in one bed.
Bizan doesn't know what to think now Parviz has gone.
What is possible that Sara can buy?
Sara must have medicine.
Her daughter is making a necklace
She is making it for her sister
She is upset
She is missing Parviz

Their house has fallen down
There were turquoise bees and jasmine honey
But now there are no trees and there are no flowers and no honey.

John must go to the conference but he has postponed it until tomorrow.

His life depends upon it.

John must not fuck it up thought Mary

But it is fucked up.

Mary had stopped telling her husband the truth

She had never been to a biscuit conference
Some arsehole up there telling you all about biscuits, but more about
        how to sell them

She didn't think she was cheating on her husband

Who gives a fuck?

They have a lifetime's supply of biscuits.

It's not easy to saw down a large tree when the wind is howling through a forest.

In her bedroom Poppy wrote a letter to her Aunt in such a wind.

"I have killed a mad dog with a sharp stick from the forest." Who knows?

That day a paper airplane landed next door – with enough energy and fecundity we can secure the future.

Poppy told her Aunt to keep all of her money in her drawer.

The banking crisis had certainly taught some people new tricks.

I sat under a tree of Walnut smoking a cigarette watching the new arrivals disembark from the paper plane.

They certainly knew how to throw a party.

The sky became dark with cloud and the trees shook with the power of the rain.

Refreshments and drinks were being served. I crossed over the wooden bridge to get a closer look.

They were all getting rather far too carried away on self-indulgent hedonistic flights.

Thankfully they were digging holes for themselves.

I knew Poppy would never answer my question about the dead dog. I wondered if she would bury it.

A Spanish Journey

everybody I see is you, like an Alex Katz, their heads stuck in space, their
     bright eyes

cut off at the neck

but it can't be

you are old and have a stick and red pants

my head is red paint

what goes through it is blind red panic

I criss-cross the Boulevard de Strasbourg on red sticks and a bandage

you wear tight jeans and make-up it can't be you and your hair

your hair ties up a heaven, I have a deranged look and claw my face

can somebody help me

all the pills are white, pastillas.

I forget the message in a bottle

my head is a pile of mush – you are looking straight through me –

he has an ego like a tall tower in an old skyline,

flux, exhaust and erectile confidence

it's half past four and I'll tear this up, snowflakes, polish coal, crocodiles,
        hums

they want him to identify the bodies of his family

blue shoes, bodice, photograph

it all ends in a sewer

a city about to implode under the weight of what needs

spreading satrapies from horizon to horizon

torn into a sandstorm of brain activity, order in disorder, just about

what was it you wanted

what was it you ever wanted

Ben Gunn as Simeon Stylites

to be happy to brush the hair from your brow

in a picture in a moment for one second

hovering over your unsaid thoughts

shaped by the wind and ugly buildings which will not feed or clothe
        anyone

we don't live in the city or wear pinched shoes but the radio is universal

we watched the tv in Basque

it's all we do and take medicines

a farmer in his field

a chopped up prostitute in the river Nervión

I weary of it

I too am a tourist but I haven't seen the Dalmatian coast

I wonder why I'm looking at art or reading this poem

there's a list of names of all those who died in Treblinka

Lee Miller next to Picasso and a Sigmar Polke

"where are the testicles?"

and they blame it on emissions

let us question the cake, the icing

let us ask of the nuts that they be tasteful the raisins plump and
        the sultanas fat

full of the sun

she knows of these fruits in her making

she knows of the past and the future (it is negligible, you will find under
        the sky, a mist, a veil, a latticed shadow on teeth)

the sun red and yellow, the sun orange, orange on a field of green and
        yellow sage

yellow on the fields of mustard

the sun girdles the fields of lemon and lace

the mouth and tongue carry the sweetest of cakes

it is frosted it has ice

to live out of this world

with only a few cloves, some cinnamon, walnuts and
a slice

the sun ripened red and yeast the colour of yam on her thigh

late summer early dew on the fields
a sky still full of stars

it melts down the lead of the heart

the stones in a heavy chest

and the size of a mountain that hangs on the wall

flies hover on the hem of a breeze

a Muscovy duck goes by in a boat to get beauty

alive with fresh peckings

I wish I had a little hat like that

some people are like cold fish

with their gold rings, cold creams and fish paste

sleet across Wendy Bergman's face in a

blancmanged landscape like drops of couscous and bird shit

her hair is forest thick her lips are cherry chapped

do fish have a memo – short fin like dabs of place, a comma of

dandruff over a mountain peak

she walks through volcanic ash in another language

once in a different frame (of mind) the wolf de la Vega counts his chickens

he has one Fluffy, one Flossie and one Tandorri

the ash moults like snow to softly cover our loss

motes in the mind dust in the luft

They hung noodles on the white-thorn to dry

he would add noodles to his horse-feed

drunk they ran through the streets pan tossing a tofu dish

scallops the colour of pearls, seaweed rice

later they watched over the sheep

eating out of a huge bowl cut from a rose wood tree

trees hover over the bay

box trees are good for horses

they run along the beach and out into the water

elasticated they thought they would come back to life

a pop-out cork from a coffin with a shoe horn

the seeds of tress in the fruit

the delicious plum in the fridge

A Short Novel

somewhere lovely in the rain with a picture by a famous florist
with a damper on to fuel his flame
it has the atmosphere of a bad restaurant
a man cleaning plate
a lintel and a door space
and Anna who rejects money, sex & being wife
on the following day of *It is* a dog comes to Anna
with a brag of honey
blown by the ill wind of fortune
he shoots her
maybe in Uruguay with its extraordinary rates of literacy

DOLON THE TROJAN

A WOLF-SKIN AND A WEASEL CAP

DOLON AND A TOASTIE AND THE KING OF THRACE

you complain (a song) about poached pears

COTTON YEW, entrails and entails

and a work called *Droomboek*

that I've forgotten you

stabbed by spears like a winkle

you take up many tissues

TIS SUES TIS SUES

hiding themselves in the bodies of the dead

Two Paintings in the Uffizi

I stared into the sheep's eyes
and the golden rope
that came out of the sky into his hands

was it Cosimo?

there was a small Pope
performing on the trampoline and flying

it's a long corridor
but you can gaze at the Arno

uprooting him from his life
pulling back his hair and cutting his throat

and a wave passed over me

Assisi

only remnants of their clothes remain
not the true cross or a shard of bone or his little penis

of no use

poor Clare

his hands tremble and shake but his eyes glint in the Leonardo da Vinci

to open up the stomach and read the signs

I can tell by the way you walk that nothing works,

her hip sets off the metal detector

collect your change (the life to come)

it wasn't me who spoke to the animals telling them to fuck right off

a town plagued   by wolves and litter

and up on the hill a cross by Giotto

kicking the water dispenser before we leave for good luck

I watched the weather forecast over France

summer rain   it could be life changing

for many

marching across Paris in galoshes

a million books on how to die
        t   (the soul?)

you reach a point where's there's no return
and the clarity we search for is finally
only a clear blue sky
if you're lucky

even if the day is wet and cloudy

you will lay awake waiting for me, worrying

back to back atoms aching to be as one

I read your book knowing how old fashioned you were

or were they slippers

a small step outside, unaided, is a relief
gray and we manage coffee — a chain of events occur
I destroy my notebooks
take up ballroom dancing
fly fishing
zip coding
the idea that one can do / accomplish anything, but "my leg"
clumsy piano playing (no reference)
and the distant mists and balms of K2
the moon from space
driving me through the night, winter rain and gusts,
protein supplements the colour of Australian sunsets
Swimmers at Gallipoli,
a dead crow on the road
a stick of wormwood

Since in a net I seek to hold the wind

a siskin and then a bunting
two killers in a red circle
the cop (*un flic*) knows everyone, is bad

I am not catholic but it rains
Jean-Pierre holds his Stetson in a January wind

they rip buds and pick nuts

the (stolen) diamonds are stuffed into a holdall

you are my angel in the wind
noli me tangere
you restoreth my soul

four pills and a tube of ointment
is all it takes

Paris by moonlight, Spain by train, film by Melville

The train leaves Austerlitz, Paris to Lisbon
Hendaye, Irun, San Sebastian
It's in *Fiesta* where Hemingway catches a train to Spain for *la corrida*
We depart from Montparnasse where on the platform I'm having a diet
      coke without you
Partly because you're not there
Partly because there are no other sugar free drinks
It's raining in San Sebastian
much like the beginning of *Un Flic*
and I talk with a street seller
He directs me to the la farmacia
where I buy pain killers

Cathy is young and very attractive
as is Alain Delon
who is too keen and quick to exploit the vulnerable

a toy train moves through our dark night

later there is a documentary about Arik Sharon

built like a barrel and in love with the bulldozer

After the square

after the Roman era fell
the manner of its creation was forgotten

the word *wedjet* signifies blue

but the sky over me is a dome
silver foil shakes in the breeze

birds, bats

I sit down by the fire and heat my can of pees

a decorative French sofa,

a relish of purees blown by the wind, a pull ring

there are just so many hours in the week in which

swimming in the Red Sea

and a gateaux layer upon layer of calories

Here

here come the planes

you collapse to the floor

do spiders eat their young?

I'm done with decorating

the front of the building is missing

an open wound

going up in puffs of smoke

burns to the face, arms, a missing foot

in the time of Pompey in the land of Judea

you can't see a thing

your arms shake with black spots

don't worry you say, don't worry

there is a rush of blood

piss on the bathroom floor

Come

your stick is made to measure

siege warfare

pouring oil over supplicants

your carers wear green tops

you see ants and stars at the top of the stairs,
re-cognition in the valley

a winding stream

of piss across the bathroom floor

a woman screams for her family

but there are none

a small group of men (mainly) in advance with an icon

the *res publica* gone to shit

fluttering

too late to hit the panic button

The

floored, you feel pinned to it

your heart rate is up in your chest

the sky is purple and there's a storm

float

cling to water

catch the relief parcel

you are bruised all over

drink

and they are flushing the system

underfloor heating, soundproofing

you can't see to open the tin

tuna friendly pain killers

blood thinners, diuretics

panegyrics

eulogies

here come the planes

Planes

throw the house plants out

the dust

the trees in the Orto Botanico near the Villa Farnesina
curatives

and the wind bringing water to your eye

is it far to go

the gate with the little booth

eating their sandwiches

little angels waiting on the steps
to welcome you, you hope

you wouldn't think it all so near, just a step away

over the river

to the cimitero

Take This Hand

figs this year and next?

who knows?

their sacks full of apples and pears

where did it all begin?

I sit in the cinema and for a moment I'm not here

alka seltzer skies dissolve

figs from your neighbour

but the tree has long gone

your hands shake and you need a straw

you don't go much on the colour

and the air from the open window is all you need

just give me a moment

and when all others are sheltering from the elements

you don't have night-vision or daylight hours

you scratch where your arm hurts

ours

and the struts are exposed where you walk

take this hand

and hold it in yours

Lightning Source UK Ltd.
Milton Keynes UK
UKOW02f1242160215

246348UK00002BA/75/P